Hello
Mama, Hello
Papa

Hello Mama, Hello Papa

Willy Breinholst

adapted by
Richard O'Brien

PUBLISHED BY POCKET BOOKS NEW YORK

Another *Original* publication of POCKET BOOKS

POCKET BOOKS, a division of Simon & Schuster, Inc.
1230 Avenue of the Americas, New York, N.Y. 10020

ISBN: 0-671-47924-5

First Pocket Books trade paperback printing August, 1984

10 9 8 7 6 5 4 3 2 1

FOREWORD

Hi, Mom. . . . Hi, Dad. . . . Hi, world! Look at me! I'm writing a *foreword*! I'll bet you think I'm just the usual diaper-draped dynamite—a bloodcurdling yowler up top, and a complete lack of consideration down below. Well, you're right. But I'm also more than that—a lot more! Maybe you can't tell by looking at me, but, believe me, it's guys just like me who in a few years will be up to our ears in the job of changing countries, kingdoms and cities; building bridges, speeding through the universe in big space laboratories, playing beautiful music and writing great books. You get me now, right? You've got to take good care of me, and bring me up right, to keep me from turning into one of those kids you wouldn't want me to play with, or, even worse, one of those adults *you* wouldn't want to play with!

I'll bet you wonder sometimes: What do you suppose that little twerp is really thinking? Well, read on, MacDuff. I think about *everything* this little book reveals . . . and much, much more.

I wonder where I really came from. It's sure got everybody guessing.

WHERE'D I COME FROM?

I don't think anyone really knows where I came from. To tell you the truth, I hadn't ever bothered thinking about it, because as far as I was concerned, I'd always simply been here. But I guess not, because today my big brother pulled on Mommy's skirt and said, "Ma, in nursery school today the teacher asked if we knew where little kids come from, you know, like my baby brother. And someone said a stork brings them. And then someone else said all you have to do is buy a big bag of baby seeds at the drugstore. I went with the guys who said the stork."

"Come on," Mommy answered back. "You know perfectly well where your brother came from, don't you?"

"Well, sure . . ."

"So? Why didn't you tell them?"

"Because I didn't want to have to admit my brother is just homemade."

I've already been around a little too long.

I'M AS LONG AS I AM!

Sometimes we go to an office that has a man who behaves very, very strangely. Without even asking permission, he picks me up, slaps me down on a scale and measures how long I am. Weird, right? So naturally, I start to cry. Doesn't the man understand kids are as long as they're supposed to be? You don't need a ruler to tell that! But I guess he just doesn't have any manners, let alone sense. I wonder what he'd do if I turned *him* bottom up in the air, and weighed and measured him? I bet he'd cry even more than *I* do!

He also talks with my mother about what I should eat. He says I have to eat healthy stuff. Naturally, since he's weird, none of the junk he says is healthy tastes any good. My mother has a funny nickname for him. She calls him "The Doctor." Today my big brother came along, and The Doctor asked him if he was happy to have me. He said he didn't know.

"Would you rather exchange him for a little sister?" The Doctor asked.

"Are you out of your gourd?" my big brother asked. "You can't do that! He's already used!"

Boy, am I pampered!

DIAPERS ARE DUMB!

I guess I shouldn't come on like an expert or anything—at least not yet—but in my humble opinion, an awful lot of time gets wasted by turning my bottom up in the air when I have to be changed. What takes up all that time are the idiotic diapers my parents take off and put on me. It takes them forever to change me. Oh, sure, I like my bottom dried off when it's wet, but there must be a better system than diapers! My father thinks so, too. He'll never win the Nobel Prize for diaper changing. Last night, when he was struggling with a great big glob of doo-doo in my diaper, which got on my bottom, my stomach, my back—actually, almost all over me!—he had to quit and call in my mother. And then he said something that couldn't have been truer: "Sure, it's great that they can send men to the moon," he groaned, "but what'll blow my mind is when they invent a baby who poops nothing but nice, dry, odorless pellets! After all, if goats can do it, why not babies?"

If I weren't such an understanding guy, what he said would've got *my* goat!

All I'm doing is keeping abreast. . . .

I'M A BREAST-FED BABY!

I'm a lucky guy. I'm a breast-fed baby. My father says that if it's at all possible, a baby should get its food directly from the source. No middle man. Mother's milk, he says, is the most wholesome nourishment a little guy like me can have. Cow's milk can't come close to mother's milk. You don't have to wait in line in the store for mother's milk; you don't have to pay for it; you don't have to put it in the refrigerator; you don't have to heat it up and, last but not least, the container for mother's milk is a hell of a lot more shapely than a carton of milk! That's what he says.

"Just stop," my mother giggles whenever my father really get going on all the advantages. He's always so interested in the whole process whenever I eat. I think he sometimes wonders what it would be like to get food the way I do. Just before, when I was eating, he suddenly said, "It must feel like sticking your head into warm pudding while you're reaching for a brew!"

What's a little "napper" supposed to do?

MY AFTERNOON NAP

I'm going through a bad period. The problem is my afternoon nap. It doesn't work, and that's because I don't know what I'm supposed to do when they put me in the baby carriage and wheel it outside. I lie there wide awake, and then I drop my pacifier. Then I start bawling. That works! They come running out to give me my pacifier again. On a good day, I can spit it out as often as seventeen times. I know because my mother kept count. Lying there like that, I get so bored I even cry a little, but at least there's a lot I can get them to do. For example, I can get them to push the carriage back and forth, back and forth! It really feels nice and comfortable, even though sometimes it *does* make me fall asleep. I can also get them to give the whole thing up and take me out of the carriage without my having had my nap—whatever that is. But when they do that, it turns into a very bad day. I get on their nerves, according to them. Well, so what? It's up to them to see that I don't get cross. What kind of day will it be today? I don't know. My mother just peeked very, very carefully into the baby carriage at me. Just a teeny-tiny quick look. To be perfectly honest, a sneaky look.

"Shhhhh . . . I think he's sleeping."

Then she tiptoes back to our house. That's okay with me. I prefer to wait and throw my pacifier out of the carriage and start crying just as she's all the way back to the house.

They don't catch *me* napping!

You can adapt to a lot of things in life—even milk in a bottle.

I HIT THE BOTTLE

It all began with my mother not having enough food for me anymore. She just couldn't manage to get properly filled up. I sucked and sucked and sucked, but nothing came out. So then they started pushing a bottle at me, and even though there was lots of yum-yum coming out of the nipple on the bottle, somehow there was something missing—something soft to nestle my head against comfortably while I ate. A bottle's not exactly something you can snuggle with. I mean it's hard! But I suppose you can get used to a lot of things in life. Because I *have* gotten used to it. Oh, I almost forgot to say I've also changed milk suppliers, at night anyway. When I cry because I'm hungry, it's my *father* who gets up and delivers the goods. He shuffles sleepily into the kitchen, makes all sorts of clatter, then comes back to me like a sleepwalker, carrying a warm bottle full of all that yum-yum. While I'm enjoying my meal, he sits on a stool and sways back and forth with his eyes closed, strictly Dullsville. But sometimes he's fun anyway. Like last night when he kept swaying and swaying—and then suddenly fell of the stool!

"Ah-ooohhhh," I said.

That means whoops.

Daddy said whoops another way, but I'm not allowed to talk like that.

Will what happens to the soap happen to *me?*

WHEN AM I CLEAN ENOUGH?

My big brother and I agree on one thing: It's really dopey, having to get cleaned up all the time. My mother and father never stop washing me. I just hope they don't wash me completely away. See, when they wash me, they also wash the soap. And I've noticed that each time they wash it, it gets smaller and *smaller*. That *alone* can make you nervous about all their washing. My big brother never wants to come in and get washed up when my mother calls him. "I don't need to be clean when I'm gonna play with my friends," he says. "We know each other by our voices!"

Besides, my brother never puts his dirty hands on the doors. He kicks them open. And when he came out of the bathroom just a minute ago, my mother asked him how his hands got so dirty.

"They got dirty," he explained, "when I washed my face!"

Yesterday when he was out playing in mud puddles, our next-door neighbor asked him how old he was.

"Four," he said.

"Imagine that!" she said. "To think a boy can get so dirty in just four years!"

That's the last time I chug-a-lug!

OOOHH, I FEEL TERRIBLE!

Ooohh, do I feel awful! Ooohh, do I feel terrible! I just drank my milk more quickly than usual. *All* of it. I emptied the whole bottle in almost one gigantic gulp when my father handed it to me. Because you see, he did the same with a bottle of something else in it. "Cheers," he said as he held his bottle up to his mouth, and let the liquid glug, glug, glug down his throat. And so we chug-a-lugged it, both of us. It was fun, guzzling along with my father. But do I feel terrible now! It must be something I ate, because my stomach feels like it's all blown up and is too big for my body, and the elastic in my pants feels like it's about to snap. I feel like I have a bellyache and also as if I want to say something, although I can't figure out what it is. The only thing that's for sure is that I feel terrible in my stomach, or someplace down there. I don't have any idea what's wrong, but if something doesn't happen soon . . . BURP!

That was it!

Ooohh, and did it help.

I'll have to remember that one.

I'm going to leak the news to you.

I'M LEAKY!

There's something wrong down in my diaper area. My mother says it's diaper rash and comes from ammonia in the diaper. She doesn't know what she's talking about. Sure, I may have a red behind and, yes, I'm really chafed, but absolutely no one but me knows why I have a red bottom. I have it because I suffer from chronic leakiness. Ever since I've known myself, I've been springing leaks. And no one does anything about it! Sure, they change my diaper lots, but that doesn't stop the leaking at all. Because suddenly I'm leaky again and my mother and father feel around to see how leaky I am and then they say, ""#@#%$&0¢$% are you wet again?!"

You bet I'm wet again. It's real easy when you're as leaky as I am. You know, when the roof gutter was leaking, my father said he could take care of it with a little patching. And he did, and it doesn't leak anymore. So what about me? Nobody thinks of making *me* watertight with any kind of patching.

But I guess my problem's not that unusual. Just a minute ago, on the radio, I heard the president complaining about all the leaks in Washington.

I wonder if they blame it on the ammonia in *Washington's* diapers?

Child rearing's kid stuff!

CHILD REARING . . . HA!

I think I'm about to figure out something. I'm about to figure out what they mean by child rearing. I think child rearing is when parents try to bring their children up to do the exact opposite of what their children feel like doing. I've also figured out that it's my mother who does most of my child rearing. My father doesn't feel like using half as many words to say all the things I mustn't do. "Oh, what the hell. . . ." is all he says when I've done something wrong which has made my mother very angry. My grandmother and grandfather also practice child rearing on me whenever they have to take care of me. But I'm not one bit afraid of them. Of course, they do get just a bit cross when I make a really great doo-doo two seconds after they've changed my diaper! That's something they're not completely ready to cope with, I guess. So then they get these deep wrinkles on their foreheads and practice child rearing on me. But pretty soon they forget what they've been talking about.

Then we just have lots of fun again.

When you get right down to it, I'm pretty good at grand-parent rearing.

You can't blow smoke rings from a thumb.

A FUNNY NEW SUCKING GAME

Sometimes I pretend to quit sucking and make believe I'm smoking cigars just like my father. I stick a finger in my mouth and smoke it; you know, inhale and exhale and all that. *Exactly* like my father. But it doesn't taste that good. And I'm disappointed that it doesn't taste better because both my mother and father say that soon I'll be too big for my yummy pacifier.

So with that gone, what's left? Anything else besides cigars? Well, cigarettes, of course. My mother smokes them. And if she does, they must be healthy; she's always saying that I'm supposed to eat mashed carrots and mashed spinach and every kind of really healthy stuff. But, personally, I think cigarettes are best for pulling out of their package and breaking them into a lot of tiny pieces. When I've completely torn a whole package apart, it always get discovered. Then my mother scolds me while she scrapes all the shreds of tobacco and pieces of paper together. It's not fair. She never gives me the chance to put the cigarettes back together again and then stuff them neatly back into the package.

Hey! It just occurred to me! And this is *really* scary. What if, when they take away my pacifier, they also take away my *thumb*?

But they do taste a lot better than cigars.

MY THUMB TASTES YUMMY!

Now I have it all in black and white. Actually, it's sort of a drama. My father's on my side; my mother's on her own side, and it all revolves around my thumb. My left one. It's the main character in the whole very dramatic story.

I shouldn't suck on it, my mother says. But my father found something in a book about babies and he read it out loud to my mother: "Recent studies have shown that when the infant sucks on its fingers, it is not a manifestation of a habit, but of a need." In other words, go ahead and suck! So now the subject's been dropped for a while. But if I know my mother, she'll pick it up again the minute she finds a book which says that the most recent studies show that finger sucking is a bad habit after all. And the wheel of fortune'll spin again. But until then, I'll just have a nice, cozy time with my thumb. My thumb tastes almost as good as real yum-yum. It's strange . . . I've tried sucking on the other fingers, too, and I've even tried to put my whole hand in my mouth. But no matter how I twist and turn them, my recent studies prove that all the flavor is in the thumb!

If any thumb manufacturers want a testimonial, tell them to give me a call.

I'm not always a good audience.

MY GRANDFATHER IS FUN!

Sometimes I stay overnight at my grandmother's and grandfather's. If I've already used up all my sleep during my nap, I can't sleep when they put me to bed at night. So I start to wail with all my might and then the show begins! My grandfather shows me how he can wiggle his ears and how he can make bblbbl-bblbbl-bblbbl-bblbbl noises by flipping his fingers up and down over his lips. In the olden days, he used to let me listen to his watch, but now he says I've become bored by tick-tock sounds. So instead he does animal acts—tearing around the whole bedroom, flapping his arms and acting like a cluck-cluck hen and a baa-baa sheep and an oink-oink pig. He expects me to laugh, the big showoff. But, of course, I can't, because I'm not finished crying. I never finish crying until they take me out of bed, and I get my grandfather to play horsey so I can take a long ride on his back all over the whole house. When he kicks out one of his back legs and whinnies, I think it's funny, and then I laugh.

From kids my age, you can't expect a high degree of sophistication.

A man can never have too many pacifiers.

IS MY PACIFIER FOOLISH?

My mother and father have started a really dumb game. I can't figure out the reason for it. The way I figure it, they're just out to annoy me—lots! But whenever they start it, I begin bawling so spectacularly that I should get a medal for it. What happens is, they take my pacifier away from me. Well, excuse me, but I don't see what's so funny about that. They say I shouldn't lie around sucking on that dumb pacifier. "Yuk," they say. "Tastes bad-bad." Then they take it away and I scream just as loud as I can. "Tastes good-good," I scream. But they don't understand. Still, I do end up getting my pacifier back every time. And when I get it, I don't feel like crying anymore. I just suck on it and feel really great—until they come back the next day and try to pull the same stupid trick on me all over again My mother read in a book about a child's first year of life: "It is easy to break the habit of the excessive use of pacifiers." Well, I flatly disagree with the lady who wrote the book. In any event, I intend to keep on testing her theory. Oh no . . . my mother just came in and took away my pacifier.

"Waaaaaaaaaaaaaaaaaaaaaaaaaahhhhhhhhhh!!!"

Ha! Another theory dented. Thanks for the pacifier, Mom.

Most water's good.

WATER SPLASHING IS FUN!

There're lots of good kinds of water. The best water, though, is the kind you splash with. I also really like the kind of water in water glasses on the table that you can tip over by tugging a little on the tablecloth. My big brother loves the kind of water that collects outside in puddles that he can jump into so it splashes out in every direction. But the water my big brother loves best of all is the kind you mix with dirt to make mud pies and smear all over your head.

I really like the water in my bathinet, but not right away. Sometimes, when they put me in it, I cry a little bit at first. But pretty soon after, when I sit in the middle of the water and try to drown all my toys or teach them to swim, I think it's lots of fun. Then I don't want to get out—at least, not before I've splashed all of it onto the floor.

Actually, there's only one kind of water I hate. It's the water they use to wash me with. What a waste of perfectly good water!

What's in a name?

WHO AM I?

When people ask my mother what my name is, she tells them, but it's a name I never hear otherwise. My mother calls me "My Little Darling" or "Sweetie-pie" or "Dumpling," and my father calls me "Slugger" and "Big Boy" and "Dynamite." My brother doesn't call me any of those things. He calls me "Jerk" and "Brat" and "Hey." I like it best when he calls me "Hey," because as soon as he calls me that he thinks of a good game for us to play. Like when he breaks something and then gives me the pieces to hold. We think it's a great game, but Mommy doesn't. Sometimes I think mothers don't know anything about playing games. Anyway, my grandmother calls me "Precious," and my grandfather calls me "The Little Feller" and "Squirt." I don't understand why they ever gave me a name in the first place, since nobody ever uses it. Maybe names are just for telling to people when they ask what your little boy's name is. It saves a lot of time. Otherwise my mother would have to answer, "My Little Darling Sweetie-pie Dumpling Slugger Big Boy Dynamite Jerk Brat Hey Precious The Little Feller Squirt." After all that, she'd be too tired to feed me!

Some guys just know how to have fun.

I GET ON MY MOTHER'S NERVES!

Sometimes my mother really gets uptight. And completely without reason, because it's definitely not me there's something the matter with. It's my mother's problem. My father says she's too involved in her role as a mother. My grandmother says she doesn't get enough sleep. My other grandmother says she's too tense. My aunt says it's a vicious circle, with a nervous mother and a screaming baby. For instance, she says, look at what happened to the gravy bowl. My goodness, it's not the only gravy bowl in the world!

My aunt was absolutely right. What happened to the gravy bowl was nothing to get hysterical about. All I did was pull a little teensy bit on the tablecloth so the bowl, which was full of gravy, dropped onto our new carpet. I didn't say it, but I felt like saying, "Ooh, see! Big blop all over the floor! I sure am a fun guy!"

But my mother got completely hysterical and screamed and all that stuff. "I can't take anymore of this!" she shouted.

"It's all nerves," my father whispered to my grandmother. And then they got very quiet while they waited for my mother to stop ranting. She couldn't tolerate the least bit of noise, I guess. Finally, my grandmother got a bottle of aspirin and tried to make her take one.

"Okay," she finally gave in, "but stop making all that noise pulling out the cotton!"

Time for a one-baby show.

WILL I BE ANOTHER PICASSO?

It could be that I'm going to be an artist when I grow up. My father says I have an inborn talent. Maybe I'll be another Picasso or Van Gogh, he says. I don't know who they are. I don't think they live in this house. But anyway, my father said so while my mother was wiping my artwork off the wall. I had painted it with a jar of red jam, which I'd heaved onto the floor along with the tablecloth. I really like strong colors. But I think my mother would just as soon my artistic abilities got inhibited. She sort of gave that impression as she scraped up the little bit of jam I hadn't used. My big brother draws and paints a lot in nursery school. Today he came home and told us that the teacher asked him to draw something completely backwards. For example, a dog pulling a man on a leash, or a canary keeping an old lady locked in a cage. That kind of thing.

"So what did you draw?" my mother asked.

"Something really neat," my big brother answered. "I drew the little brat powdering Dad's behind!"

Sitting pretty . . . if a little puzzled.

NOW I CAN SIT ON THE POTTY!

My mother and I have started on what I guess is a circus act. I can't explain what the idea of it is, but it's heaps of fun. Once in a while they put me on something called the "potty." Without diapers or pants on. And then they say, "Make doo-doo!"

And then I sit there and chuckle to myself and just generally have a good time. Sometimes my mother or my father lifts me a little and peeks way down into the potty. "Hm, he hasn't made any doo-doo at all," they say. "Let's try again, kid. Come on, big, big doo-doo!"

And they go on like that for a long time. Finally, they don't feel like it anymore and then they put diapers and pants back on me, put the potty away and look very disappointed. And then I think, "It's sad for my mother that the potty won't make that doo-doo!"

And so, to please her, I make one myself in my diaper.

A great big one.

Call the *Guinness Book of World Records*. . . .

FUN TOYS

I have to admit I've tasted better things than my mother's coral red lipstick. But, on the other hand, I won't say no thank you, no more lipstick for me! Because, see, you can have a lot of fun with lipstick. Not only can you paint your whole face and head with it, you can paint the blanket and the pillow. I don't think there are many babies my age who have prettier blankets than the one I had yesterday after I was finished with my mother's lipstick. I ate a little of it, too. But I didn't like it, so I spit it out again. And then my mother came in. She screamed and rushed out to get my father.

Sometimes she reacts a little strongly, and over the silliest things! It's certainly nothing to make such a big fuss about. I mean, I know for a fact that she has more than just one lipstick. But there was trouble anyway, and even though they kept on washing me the whole rest of the day, it didn't help much. I was still coral red all over. Something about being kissproof, even though no one had kissed me.

"Actually, I don't think it's that bad," my father said. "There've been black, white and yellow babies since the dawn of time. But, until now, never a coral red one!"

Lookin' good.

A REALLY DUMB GAME

My mother and father play a really dumb game. Well, it's actually my father who mostly plays it. I can't really say there's any point to it because I'm sure there isn't any. It has something to do with them suddenly saying I'm supposed to look happy, and then my father holds a little black box up in front of his face so you can hardly see him. Then all at once there's a really bright light, the box goes CLICK! and then nothing more happens. That is, besides my crying sometimes, because I don't like that bright light.

Then my father'll say, "That was a great shot!" or "I'll take one more while he still looks good!"

Look good? Don't I *always* look good? Doesn't a guy look the way he looks? One time my father told me to look happy as I sat on my grandfather's lap. After the box said CLICK!, my grandfather said, "Well, anyway, that's one good thing about babies. They don't run around like idiots, showing stacks of photos of their wonder-parents!"

Pacifiers also keep out yukky food.

ARE MASHED CARROTS FOOD?

My mother has started giving me another kind of food. Well, I mean it's not real food. It's something weird they call "mash." There's mashed carrots, mashed peas, mashed apples, mashed potatoes and all kinds of other mish-mash they have to smear around my face because I won't allow any of that mashed junk to get inside my mouth. I'd rather have nice warm milk. A lot of that mash they give me winds up in my nose instead, and then I howl and hit the spoon so that the rest of the mash splashes right up into my mother's face or some other neat place. But the last couple of times my mother gave me mash, some of it found its way into my mouth anyway, and I swallowed a little bit of it also. Some of it didn't taste too bad, but I'm not really sure yet. In any event, I won't ever eat any of the kind of mash they call spinach. Yuk! My mother says if I eat a lot of spinach, I'll grow up big and strong.

The only reason I can see for growing up big and strong is so that I'll be able to refuse my spinach!

I've finally figured out what to use a potty for!

MY POTTY'S BEGINNING TO WORK!

It's taken a while, but I'm gradually beginning to figure out what my potty can be used for. You can fill it with building blocks and rattle them around inside it. You can also bang around in it with your rattle and make terrific music. Or you can push it over to one of the plants my mother has on the floor and try to put the plant into it, just the way mother sometimes transplants a flower. But I haven't mastered that yet. I can only tip the plant over. Still, that's something. I can also empty my bottle into the potty, too! In other words, my potty's beginning to work. Of course, they wouldn't have invented potties if there wasn't anything they could be used for. Yesterday, when I was alone in the living room for a minute, I made terrific mud pies out of some meatballs. It all looked so pretty that when my father came in and stared into the potty, he became really excited and happy.

"Big, big boy!" he said. "Make big, big doo-doo in nice, nice potty!"

Next time I'll make him even happier and add some spaghetti.

Carpets may be an acquired taste.

TIME TO EAT

I'm involved in something my mother and father call a feeding problem. I don't really know what it's all about, but they make a big production out of mealtimes. Actually, a lot of what they try to fill me with, I don't feel like eating. But between meals, I like to eat some of the flowers in the living room, or just taste them. I also like to eat a little of my big brother's mud pies, or put some of the fringe from the carpet in my mouth and suck the juice out of it. But when I'm at the table, my mother and father get into arguments about how to get me to eat. Finally, my father says, "Here, let me!" The spoon slowly comes closer and closer to my tightly clamped mouth, and then my father says, "Umm, nice yummy stuff. You're a big boy now. See if your mouth is big enough to fit in a whole giant airplane . . . zoooommmm . . . the plane's coming into the hangar now. . . ."

Well, okay, so I open my mouth and then my father empties the spoon into it. He looks triumphantly at my mother and says, "If you'd only use a little psychology, it would go just as smoothly for *you*."

That's when I let the food ooze nice and quietly out of my mouth. All of it.

Then you should see the way my mother looks at my father. The strange things that make her happy!

I wonder why my car's beginning to rust?

I HAVE MY OWN CAR!

I have my own car. It's a Junior Baby Coupe DS-Super with fully synchronized, self-adjusting disk brakes on all four wheels, front-and-back-wheel drive, and a four-wheel suspension system. My car is cylinder-free with a semi-automatic level regulator, and genuine power steering (that is, when my father steers it), and it can reach a top speed of, I think, fifty-five miles an hour (when my father pushes it on his way to a softball game or when he comes home a little late). When we come racing down the street, children and old ladies have to run out into the road to escape the speeders. My father and me.

I also take a nap in my car. And whenever I've slept a really long time in it, a little condensed water is very likely to appear in the bottom. But aside from that, it's in fine working order . . . even if the paint is somewhat scratched and the tread on the tires has just about worn down and there is a little rust here and there. After all, I've inherited it from my big brother. My father says that it won't pass the next inspection.

"But *you* will, Dynamite," he adds.

From time to time, I can use a little reassurance like that.

It's not a sweater. It's an OW-er!

SWEATERS ARE A PAIN!

I've gone from diapers and little shirts into play pants. As far as I'm concerned, we can darn well go back to the diapers and shirts. I can't see the point of play pants because there are some annoying knitted pullovers that go with them. It's my grandmother who knits them with yarn that comes from a ball which rolls around on the floor. Every time I visit her, I have to try on a sweater. In trying it on, I always have to stick my head through a hole in it, and that's not exactly fun, not at all. My grandmother doesn't have enough sense to knit holes big enough for my head to go through without it hurting, so that I usually cry a little. "You're growing awfully fast, my precious!" she always says. What's so terrible about that? Yesterday, when I had to try on a new pullover, I absolutely couldn't get my head through the hole. My nose got squashed flat before we succeeded. "Goodness!" my grandmother said, with a look of disbelief on her face. "We haven't stuck your face through one of the buttonholes, have we?"

I've formed this really deep theory. I only have to wear knitted jackets and sweaters when my mother's cold.

If they don't get me off this potty soon, they'll be sorry. I'll go pee-pee in it.

I'M A BIG BOY!

I'm a little bit sorry about being leaky. My mother and father and big brother, they're not nearly as leaky. But they don't do anything about my leakiness. At least, nothing I think is worth anything. And they could save themselves all their trouble with that diaper nonsense, because it just plain doesn't help. One day when a water pipe down in the cellar was leaky, boy, they had to have a man come in a hurry to put in a new pipe that wasn't leaky. But even though he was here already, they didn't have him come and look at me. And despite the fact that my mother and father have recently become very interested in my leakiness. I have to get used to the potty, they say. Whenever I make a lot of widdle on the carpet where it seeps nicely away, they get upset. But when I widdle only a little bit in the potty, they stand there and praise me to high heaven, and tell me I'm a big boy. They praise me even if it's only seven drops in that dumb potty. Personally, I think I'll be an even bigger boy when I can make the whole carpet wet.

Bored.

TEETHING TROUBLES

Sometimes I lie here at night and don't really know what I'm supposed to do. But when I lie here for a while and begin to get bored, I call for my mother and father to come. They say I'm babbling. When they don't come, then I sound the alarm: "Waaaaahhh!" *That* brings them in, but by then I'm cross. And even though they take me in their arms and walk back and forth with me in the bedroom, I just go on crying because I feel so cross. They say it's because I'm teething. They can say whatever they want; I just go on bawling. So they try to give me food, and when that doesn't help they give me a clean diaper, and when that doesn't help they try to give me some toys. By that point all I do is keep on crying. Didn't you ever have one of those nights when you just didn't want to be helped?

Do I get time off for good behavior?

A PLAYPEN'S NOT MY THING!

My mother says a playpen has lots of advantages. "Whenever I work in the kitchen," she said, "I could take the playpen with me. Then I'd know where he was." So they bought a playpen for me. It's awful. The first time they lifted me up and put me into it, I howled with all my might. There were bars around my playpen! If there weren't any bars, it wouldn't be so bad. They claim I'll get used to it, but I'm not so sure about that. The worst thing is, I can't get to my toys. I throw them out of the playpen and then I have to cry to get them back again. Then, when they take me out of the playpen, they forget about my toys, and then I have to cry again, to get my toys *out*. Nope, a playpen's just not my cup of tea. A while ago, when I cried because I wanted to get out, my father lifted me up and said, "Hey, playpens are great! You should be *happy* in there."

If he really likes that playpen so much, why doesn't *he* move into it?

Pretty nice guy. But not nearly as handsome as I am.

AM I A TWIN?

Maybe I'm a twin. I really can't figure it out. All I know is, there's something fishy going on. What it boils down to is that my twin brother won't play with me. He just looks at me. Sure, he looks happy when he sees me, and sometimes he waves a little bit just for a little while. I only see him when my grandmother or somebody like that holds me up in front of something they call a mirror. "Look," they say, "see that sweet little boy in there? Who do you think he is? Do you suppose he's your sweet little twin brother? Come on . . . wave to him!"

Well, okay, so I wave a little. And *he* waves a little, too. But then I don't feel like doing it anymore, and it turns out that my twin brother doesn't feel like doing it anymore either. So then I look a little cross, and he does, too. Then when I turn around, that's it: He'll never walk around to where *I* am. Do I have a twin brother or don't I have a twin brother? Nobody who holds me up in front of the mirror gives me any kind of clue.

I'd like to have a twin brother, but not that one. He gets bored and cranky too easily. I'd like a terrific guy who's more like me.

Mabel, peel me a block!

I SET A RECORD!

I'm very touchy and irritable at the moment. I drool and gnaw on anything I can get my hands on. Toss me a box of building blocks, and I'll gnaw them into a pile of sawdust in no time. I've got "teething troubles." My mother and father stand around looking helpless, because they don't know what to do about it. "Poor little baby," my mother says, and touches my gums. It helps a little, even though I usually don't like people messing around inside my face. But if they feel around too long and too much, then I become cross and irritable and hard to get along with all over again. Then yesterday, when my father was rubbing my gums with his index finger, I got irritated . . . and bit him right on the best spot of all—right down by the root of the nail. "Ow, you little . . .!" he screamed, and called me a name I'd never heard before. Then he flew into the kitchen to my mother and shouted, "It's there, all right! He has a tooth!"

You can bet they got busy phoning the news around to everyone they knew.

From what I understand, listening to them, I'm the first baby in the world who's ever gotten a tooth.

My twin brother's a dummy.

DOUBLE TROUBLE

I've had a fight with my twin brother. You know, the weirdo in the mirror. I don't know what's the matter with him, but sometimes I think he's just out to make trouble. When I first catch sight of him in the mirror, he's nice. But he just stares. And he never answers when I speak to him. He's also stupid. I try to make contact, for instance, when I hold my pacifier out to him so he can take a taste. I'm trying to be friendly, right? But he won't taste it at all, even though I rub it all over his face. Well, that did it! We're not friends any longer. Today I smacked the mirror right down on one of my building blocks. When I looked into it again, my twin brother had run off, and had broken it besides.

And there I was, left behind in my playpen not understanding one bit of the whole thing. Of course, when my mother turned up, I got all the scolding. My twin brother kept right on hiding. He didn't want to take any of the blame, even though it was his fault.

What a little coward!

I'm a pretty spectacular eater, if I do say so myself.

NOW I EAT WITH A SPOON!

I can eat with a spoon. I just started today, with a big bunch of oatmeal. It's not as easy as it looks! My mother and father and big brother can eat with both a knife and a fork, but they don't have any fun with their food when they eat. They don't smear mash on their faces or get sauce in their hair. They just sit there—ordinary and boring—and put it all in the same old place: their mouths. But not me! My father says I'm the only baby north of the South Pole who can eat oatmeal without opening my mouth! But I don't really eat it at all. I've discovered it's much more fun to slam the spoon down into the bowl so the milk sprays out in all directions! Then my father read something in a book: "When the child begins to play with his food, then it is time to move it out of reach." So they did just that. Then I cried so hard, it was time to move the bowl back within reach. So the party wasn't over. When there wasn't anything left in my bowl, my mother and father and big brother had oatmeal in their hair and all over the place.

"Ah-mum-ah-bah-bah," I said, and threw the spoon away with—if I say so myself—real flair.

Eating with a spoon's okay, as long as you keep your mouth shut.

What're all these great toys doing in the *kitchen?*

MY FAVORITE TOYS

I have good toys and dull toys. The best toys I have, of course, are all the ones I can put into my mouth—blocks, plastic rings, that sort of stuff. Some of my teddy bears are good, too. My new rag doll, which my grandmother made, isn't bad, either. Then there are my boring toys—all the big ones which I can't throw down on the floor—they just aren't interesting at all. For some strange reason, my mother hides my favorite toys from me in the kitchen. They're in the drawer I can reach when it's pulled out a little bit. All my wonderful toys . . . stirring spoons, measuring cups, sieves, meat hammers, eggbeaters, strainers, cake utensils, can openers and all the other good things. They're all there for making a lot of noise in the drawer and for throwing on the floor. I can't understand why my mother absolutely insists on hiding my very favorite toys in the kitchen, instead of letting me keep them in my toy chest where they belong.

Sometimes my mother's not too efficient.

You'll never find me off my rocker.

MY FUNNY GIDDYAP HORSEY

I have a playmate. My mother and father call it a rocking horse. Or, more exactly, a ride-im horsey, or a giddyap horsey. You can take a long, long ride on it. A long giddyap ride, that is. When I really get riding, it tickles a little in my stomach, and then I start to laugh. But when it gets too wild, I don't want to ride and then I cry. Despite that, I really like my giddyap horsey. It's fun to have a playmate; I just wish I could take it to bed with me. Sometimes my big brother takes a ride on it, too. But he can't control it properly. It gets too wild and kicks him off. Then we laugh. Then I decide I want to ride it wildly, but I can't, because my mother says I'll cry. So to spite her, I start crying anyway, and then my horse suddenly disappears. Lots of days can go by before it comes back again. I can't figure out where it goes when it runs away. Whenever I say bop-bop-bop because I want it to come back again, my mother says that the Riding Fairy has taken it.

Who?

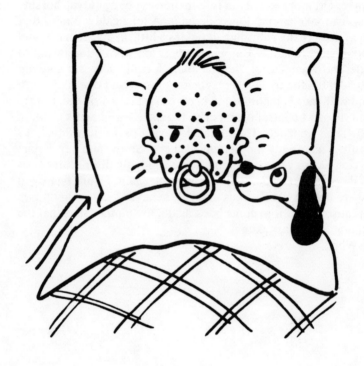

Measles make me see red!

GETTING THE MEASLES IS NO FUN!

Measles, phooey! I don't want them. My mother and I went to a man's house. He was a different man, but she called him "The Doctor," too. "It's nothing to worry about," he said, "it's the measles." After he said that, we gave him some money and went on our way, but we forgot to leave my measles with him. And I'm getting tired of them. I feel terrible. I feel so terrible I don't even feel like crying. I just lie here and feel miserable. Every time my mother and father come in and look at me, they look *so* worried, and my big brother isn't even allowed to touch me. They say he mustn't come near my bed, because he's only had the German measles. I wonder which country *my* measles come from? I don't even feel like breaking anything to bits. I just don't feel like doing anything. And now these dump measles have started to get sore behind my ears. They hid themselves there a whole day before they came out. That's what my father says. Let them go hide somewhere else. I'm sick of them.

The only thing that helps a little bit is when my mother bends over me and says, "My poor, poor little darling!"

That's a comfort.

I wish that doctor would hurry up and come get his measles.

What do you mean, to whom do I wish to speak?

I CHAT WITH THE TELEPHONE!

My mother and father call it a telephone. It's not a real, living person but they talk an awful lot with it anyway. Sometimes, when it gets bored, it becomes impatient and suddenly calls *them* . . . Ring . . . ring . . . ring . . . it goes, and then my mother or father comes dashing in and talks reassuringly to it. My mother is the one who talks best with it. Whenever she talks with it about me, it can last a long, long time. Once in a while I also try to chat with it, but I guess it doesn't really understand what I mean when I say, "Ah-bludr-ah-bludr-ah-bludr." Then it just hums, which is not exactly what I'd call a nice, cozy chat. But when I turn the dial just like my mother and father do, then sometimes it says something real. Then I say something real like, "Boo-boo-oh-di-yah-ba-ah-da-da-da-ma-goo-goo!"

After I've said a whole lot, it asks me whom I want to talk with. I want to talk with the *telephone,* of course!

Do you suppose it doesn't understand English?

My stuffed dog's not as old as I am, so I guess that's why he doesn't talk yet.

WE EACH SPEAK OUR OWN LANGUAGE!

I've started to talk. It may sound strange, but it seems that my mother, father and big brother speak a totally different language than I do. Whenever I'm hungry, I say, "Mum-mum" or "Ah-baba-baba," but my father doesn't say it like that. He says, "Damn it, isn't supper ready yet?" Whenever I have a big doo-doo in my diaper, then I say, "Ah-dooohhh-ah-dooohh" or "Adooobaaahh." Whenever my father hears that, he lights up like a bulb and yells to my mother, "I think he's trying to say Dad!" He never checks my diaper to see what it is I'm talking about. But whenever I say "Aga-bludr-ah-bludr-ah-bludr," my mother understands immediately that I'm just saying, "Aren't we having a nice time?" It's mostly when I'm getting changed and being powdered on the behind. But that's the only thing they understand. Oh, yes, they also understand when I say, "Ahooo-hhhhh." I always say that when I knock something over. I know I should say "Whoops" or "Darn it," but in my opinion, what I say sounds much more exciting. And it's always exciting to knock something over! Whenever my grandmother comes, I say, "Ah-da-da-da-da!" "Listen," she says. "He's trying to say hello!"

She doesn't understand that I'm really saying, "Here comes the one who gives me candy!"

Come on, old lady, give out the goodies.

They shouldn't give babies so many toes. There're too many to count!

MAYBE I'LL BE A NUCLEAR PHYSICIST!

I've started to develop into something my mother calls an intelligent little child. She's given me a counting thing, and I can already count and add on it. That is, only easy additions up to two, and, of course, there's no guarantee whether they're right or wrong. But it's lots of fun to sit and push the balls back and forth. If I make a wrinkle in a particular part of my forehead, my grandmother says I look "pensive." Then they all look admiringly at me and my grandfather says that I'll probably become a nuclear physicist, an economist or a director of a bank.

A few minutes ago, while I sat and pushed the balls back and forth, he said enthusiastically, "It's as plain as the nose on your face that he's sitting there doing addition. Four . . . yes, that's right . . . he's bitten me on my finger with his new tooth exactly four times!"

I hadn't realized I'd bitten him a whole four times! I thought I had bitten him a hundred thousand million thousand gillion times. But that's also a lot of times, isn't it?

And all in one day!

Whew!

Do you spell "Dear Mom and Dad" with one or two scribbles?

I CAN WRITE NOW, TOO!

I've just written an important message to my mother. And a letter to my grandmother. And a short note to my other grandmother. And a couple of memos to my father. See, I've just borrowed my big brother's pen. You know, the one that can write really black. I had so much to tell my mother that it couldn't all fit on one normal-sized writing pad. But that didn't matter. There was enough room for all of it on the wall. I used the wall my father just painted because it looked the best. And I'm really excited now about what they're going to say when they come in and read it. I can guess that my mother will say, "I'll be . . . the mail's already here!"

I'm not so sure what my father will say, but from past experience when I've written something to him on the wall, I know he appreciates it when I'm brief. And I've been just that. I've only written:

Hi, Dad . . .

Of course, with lots of hugs and kisses underneath.

For all of them.

I can't wait to say _____ and _____!

I'D SWEAR TO IT!

I'm at the diaper age, the assertive age, the nursing age and the crawling age. But what I'm really looking forward to is getting to the swearing age. My big brother has just arrived there. It's very exciting to listen to. Sometimes he says, "What the . . .!" And it's not just the first part but he says the last part, too. He's not supposed to say it because of my mother and father. My mother doesn't like his swearing at all. She says, "He'll probably wind up sounding like those awful kids on TV." Sometimes he comes over to me and tries to acquaint me with swear words that I can use someday when I get big enough.

"You must never say 'Damn it' or 'What the hell' when my mother and father are around, but once in a while when it's extremely necessary, you can say 'Darn it' or 'What the heck.' But you can get away with saying the other words sometimes. You say, 'I know I'm not supposed to say damn it! Damn it is a bad word. So it's not nice to say damn it!' "

Yesterday my big brother managed to get himself put in the corner when my mother asked him what he had done with my little red ball.

"It rolled under the sofa and went into the damned hall!" he said.

As fast as hell, they packed him off to the damned corner!

Ducks take less room in tubs than daddies.

MY FATHER'S A BOY!

My mother and father are always trying something new and exciting with me. The latest thing is giving me a bath in the big bathtub, which is really an ocean into which you get carefully put in the middle. At the beginning I put up a nice loud protest and refused, but after a while I gave in and sat right in the middle of the ocean, patting the water to make good friends with it. At first it made small waves, but they got bigger and bigger the more I patted them, which was lots of fun. My big brother always uses the big bathtub, too. He always has to have lots of boats and balls and toys with him when he takes a bath. Yesterday he had so many toys with him in the bathtub that my mother could hardly find him. She had to search a lot because of all the balls and rubber animals and everything else you can imagine. Finally, she had to shout, "Say something!" Then she found him.

So that I wouldn't get too scared the first time when I had to go into the big ocean in the big bathtub, my father went in before me. He had gotten completely undressed. And I noticed something I hadn't really noticed before. My father's a boy, just like me!

I wonder if my mother knows?

My brother wants to be two puppies.

I CAN TALK WITH ANIMALS!

I can talk with animals. And with teddy bears and dolls. I can talk with all of them. The one I talk with best is my teddy bear. He's really great, but he never wants to sleep when I take him to bed with me. He always jumps around on the covers and finally falls down onto the floor. Then, of course, I miss him and have to cry a few tears to get him back again. I also talk with animals called dogs; they sometimes lick my face, but they're hard to hold. There's a little black dog who sometimes comes and says hello to me by licking me all over my face. He's usually only allowed to say hello to me from a distance. I think he likes me because he always wags his tail when he says hello to me. He looks just like a little black dog in my big brother's animal picture book. I really like to listen when my big brother sits on my father's lap and my father reads aloud to him about all the animals. Last night he asked my big brother which of all the animals in the picture book he'd like to be.

"I'd like to be two small puppies, most of all," my big brother said.

"*Two* puppies?" my father asked.

"Yup," my big brother said. "*Two* puppies. Because then we could play with each other!"

With justice for some.

A SENSIBLE DISCUSSION

This sure is a strange world we live in. Take me, for example. It's all right for me to talk at the table, but I don't know *how* to. My big brother *knows* how to talk, but he's not supposed to do it at the table. Well, anyway, not when he's eating. But my big brother's completely hopeless about it. He can't keep quiet, especially when we have liver. He always suggests that we should send it to the poor children in India or Africa. Yesterday he wanted to know why they call it "liver" when, if you have to eat it, you want to die. And then he wanted to know if it were true that if a cannibal comes home late for dinner he gets a cold shoulder. And if there were people who sewed their old neckties into sleeping bags for snakes so they wouldn't freeze at night. And if it were true that jigsaw puzzles were invented by a Scotsman who had dropped a bank note into a meat grinder. And if pigmies are so small they have to stand on ladders to pick strawberries. He always asks these sensible questions while we're eating because he can't get them answered at nursery school.

"Please be quiet, son," my mother and father say. "You're not supposed to talk with food in your mouth."

But that doesn't stop my big brother.

"Sure, the spoiled little brat can sit there and fool around with his food and smear it in his hair and behind his ears. Isn't there any justice in this country?"

I guess not for guys who aren't spoiled little brats like me.

I just devour Shakespeare!

BOOKS SHOULD HAVE GOOD TASTE!

I don't like books much. Even picture books like the ones my big brother has so many of are really dull. None of them tastes interesting. Sure, it can be kind of pleasant to bite them a little because my gums like it, but generally books don't really grab me. Newspapers are much, much better. One, because they're easier to rip into pieces and, two, because they crackle a lot when you crinkle them. It's also a lot of fun to crawl into the hall in the morning, after the mail slot goes SMACK!, and try to rip up all the letters on the doormat. Or eat a nice little corner of one. The corner with the stamp tastes the best. Last night, after I'd eaten a big piece out of my father's newspaper, he made me spit it into his hand because he had to see what the sports scores were. When he'd smoothed out the wet scraps and was about to read what was on the paper, he got really impressed.

"Well, I'll be . . . " he said to my mother. "The kid's a genius when it comes to languages. He's chewed it into Russian!"

I wonder what language I've written his bankbook in?

Let's see. Where could they be hiding a day-care center?

WHAT'S A DAY NURSERY?

There's something I've been wondering about. Where does my father go when he goes out? Almost every single morning he leaves. I mean, instead of staying home and playing with me like my mother does. Why do I have a father at all if he just leaves? But I think he misses me a little, because suddenly when it gets to be night, he comes home and says, "Hi, Champ," and asks if I've been a good boy. And then he plays with me for a while and we have a really great time together, but next morning, darned if he doesn't go away again. And that's not the worst. It's much worse when I hear them talking about there being a place for me in something they call a day-care-center. I really can't figure that out. I mean, I'm gradually becoming familiar with the house. I know we have a dining room, a playroom, a bathroom and a bedroom. But we don't have any day-care-center room. I'm 100 percent sure of that, so how can there be a place for me in the day-care center? There's something about this whole thing that I don't like at all. Well, anyway, they won't be able to count on this kid.

No day-care center for me! I'm holding out for a place where there's lots of other little kids like me.

I'm becoming a calculating type.

I CAN ADD NUMBERS!

My father thinks a lot about my future. "Maybe he'll become an economist," he says. He's taught me to add on his calculator. It adds numbers. When I push the buttons, a whole lot of green doodles jump up on the screen. My father says that's what I've added. And it doesn't matter that I don't know if the answer is right or not; the calculator knows. I'll be adding almost as well as my big brother soon. But only almost. Today my grandfather sat my big brother up on his knee and asked him, "If I give you three red fire trucks," he said, "and your mother and father give you two red fire trucks, then how many red fire trucks would you have?"

"Six," my big brother said. My grandfather shook his head.

"No," he said, "I give you three red fire trucks and your mother and father give you two red fire trucks. How many red fire trucks do you have then?"

My big brother counted the fire trucks on his fingers.

"Six," he said again.

"Three red fire trucks and two red fire trucks. That can never make six. You'd only have five."

"No, I'd have six. Because I already have one."

My mother plays with meatballs.

I SHOULDN'T THROW MEATBALLS ON THE FLOOR!

I've finally discovered something. There are differences between people! Some people are allowed to do things that other people aren't allowed to do. Take me, for example. I mustn't play with my food at the table. Just take my meatballs, for instance. I'm practically not allowed to do *anything* with them! I'm not allowed to throw them on the floor. I'm not allowed to throw them into my big brother's bowl of soup, either. I can't whack them with my hands like the boxers on TV do. To get right down to the nitty-gritty, I'm not allowed to play with them at all. But my mother—boy, is she allowed to play with them! You should come over and watch *her!* She mixes them around in a bowl, lifts them up on a spoon, even tries to drown them in a pot of water. Later she fishes them *out* of the pot; it all looks like lots of fun. Would you believe she plays with them for more than an hour at a time? I wish I had a big pot of water for drowning meatballs, but *I'm* not allowed!

So why do they give me the dumb meatballs? If I can't use them for playing with, what good are they?

Except for chewing them to bits and then spitting them out.

There's a man hiding in this box, but I can't shake him out.

THERE ARE MEN LIVING IN OUR BOXES!

There's a man living in this box we have that my mother and father call a transistor radio. Sometimes they give it to me and I get to talk to him. "Bludr-ah-bludr-ah-bludr!" I say to him. And then he says almost the same thing—except when he plays music. There's also men living inside the two boxes we have hanging in the corners of our living room. And there's all sorts of people—whole bunches of them—living inside the big box my mother and father sit and watch at night. On the other hand, I've looked and looked and listened and listened, and now I'm absolutely certain there's nobody living in my blocks. Not in the kitchen cabinets, either—although there're knobs on the doors that you can turn. Nobody's living in my potty. The man who lives inside the transistor radio won't come out, no matter how hard I shake his box. He must really hang on tight. When I turn the knobs I can make him play different kinds of music. Just a second ago, my mother said to my father, "Go in and see what he's doing."

When my father saw me, he got all excited. "He's listening to Mozart!" he shouted. When I turned and waved to him with both hands, my father got really excited. "Now he's conducting! I'll bet he becomes another Leonard Bernstein!"

I hope not. I'd rather be *me*.

If I learn to talk any better, soon even *I* will be able to understand me!

I'VE STARTED TALKING!

It looks like I'm about to grow out of the babbling stage. My mother and father go around all day long with their ears practically twitching. I think they're waiting for me to start talking. You know, with the real words you use to spell with and write with and scold with. When my mother fed me the other day, I smacked my hand in the bowl to make my soup spread out a little more on the table. Suddenly, I said, "Omm-mmm!"

I really didn't mean anything in particular by it, but my mother went completely crazy and screamed to my father that I'd said my very first word. "He said *Mom!* So clearly!"

She was really excited. Almost as excited as my father got when he sat and played with me a couple of minutes ago. All because I said, "Da-da-da-da-da!"

You should've seen him! As fast as lightning, he zoomed over to the window and shouted down to my mother in the yard so loudly you could hear him all over the neighborhood, "He said *Dad!*"

Listen, if it makes them happy . . .

Being one year old tastes good!

HAPPY BIRTHDAY TO ME!

It was my birthday today. I don't know how old I am, but it's the first time I've had a birthday. It was fun. I got a big birthday cake with one candle on it. My father was the one who baked it, but when he put it in the oven, the candle melted. Then my mother said she'd take over. After she'd finished it, all the guests arrived. I got to taste the cake first, so I tasted it the way I like to taste things best: by smearing it all over my head. They all thought that I was a riot. Even though the candles burned my fingers, I only cried a little while my grandmother blew on them. She said it was wrong to put candles on the cake. She never has birthday candles on her own cakes. "Whenever I celebrate a birthday," she said, "it's supposed to be a party, not a torchlight parade!"

My big brother's just been to a birthday party. He came home bawling, "They said I could drink all the soda pop I wanted to, and eat all the ice cream and hot dogs I wanted to. But I couldn't—my stomach wouldn't let me!"

I guess that's why my mother sighed so much the day of *her* birthday.

What I am is perfect.

A PERFECT DAY

I've finally had a perfect day. Every minute of the day has been as smooth as peaches and cream. I didn't quarrel with my mother, not even once. I had no trouble while getting changed, no problems at all when I was supposed to take a nap, no trouble when I was supposed to eat. Not only that, I was almost able to eat with a spoon all by myself. Well, that was after I tried to eat with a fork, which wasn't successful because it was leaky. But I was almost able to eat my oatmeal with a spoon. I mean, I only got one spoonful in my ear and another in my hair. My mother said that I was on the right track! Now I just hope that I can keep on being good the whole rest of the day. My father says that I'm approaching a new world's record. I've also become much easier to manage, I think, since I started to crawl. There's so much to see and discover when you crawl around on the floor. I'm just a little bit doubtful, though, about what my mother will say when she comes in and sees that I've knocked over the vase with her brand-new flowers. But I've only eaten the red ones. The other flowers I just tore apart.

A teeny thing like that shouldn't ruin the good vibes in the house, should it?

Full and content . . . my stuffed animal . . . a fresh diaper
. . . and a dear mother and father. What more can anybody
want?

Home delivery from Pocket Books

Here's your opportunity to have fabulous bestsellers delivered right to you. Our free catalog is filled to the brim with the newest titles plus the finest in mysteries, science fiction, westerns, cookbooks, romances, biographies, health, psychology, humor—every subject under the sun. Order this today and a world of pleasure will arrive at your door.

 POCKET BOOKS, Department ORD
1230 Avenue of the Americas, New York, N.Y. 10020

Please send me a free Pocket Books catalog for home delivery

NAME _____

ADDRESS _____

CITY _____ STATE/ZIP _____

If you have friends who would like to order books at home, we'll send them a catalog too—

NAME _____

ADDRESS _____

CITY _____ STATE/ZIP _____

NAME _____

ADDRESS _____

CITY _____ STATE/ZIP _____